Understanding... Adoption

Flora's Family

Copyright © QEB Publishing, Inc. 2007

First published in the United States by
QEB Publishing, Inc.
23062 La Cadena Drive
Laguna Hills, CA 92653

www.qeb-publishing.com

Library of Congress Control Number: 2007001021

ISBN 978-1-59566-391-7

Written by Annette Aubrey
Edited by Sarah Medina
Designed by Alix Wood
Illustrated by Patrice Barton
Consultancy by David Hart

Publisher Steve Evans
Creative Director Zeta Davies
Senior Editor Hannah Ray

Printed and bound in China

Flora's Family

Annette Aubrey

Illustrated by
Patrice Barton

QEB Publishing

Flora was covered in bubbles,

having fun in a
lovely, warm bath!

Her mom and dad washed her and rinsed her
while she **shrieked**, and *giggled*, and laughed.

When Flora was all squeaky clean,
her mom dried her...

pat-a-pat, pat...

With the fluffiest,
big, yellow towel.

Then, in front of the mirror they sat.

Mom used her own special hairbrush
to brush Flora's flowing, black hair.
Flora glanced into the mirror.
Then, she stared
and she stared
and she stared.

Why's my hair so long and dark, Mom,
when yours is so short and light?
And—look!—you have all of those freckles.
I can see a lot of them there, all right!

"Let's sit with Dad," smiled her mother.
"We have something to share, sweetie.
When you were a small, tiny baby,
you became part of our family.

8

"You were a bouncy and bright-eyed baby
when we adopted you. It's true!
We loved you, dear, from the beginning,
and promised to take care of you."

Dad said, "Mom and I were delighted
to have another child to adore.
And your brother and sister were happy.
They couldn't have wanted more.

"Now, what would we do without you,
our own funny Flora, so sweet?
You are the most delightful daughter.
With you, our family's complete."

"I don't understand it," said Flora.
"Daddy, what does it really mean
to be adopted? Am I very different?
Aren't I just like Jake and Eve?"

Mom kissed Flora and hugged her.
And Dad held both Flora's hands.
"Before the day that you were born,
your birth parents made special plans."

14

And so they made a decision
that was hard and brave to do.
They chose to find a family
to **love** and to **cherish** you.

"But didn't they want to keep me?"
said Flora to her dad.

"Did I do something awful?
Did they think that I was bad?"

16

"Your birth parents wanted to know that you'd be loved and never alone. And that's what all of us wanted that day, when we brought you home.

"We're so happy now that we're a family
and we can love, and play,
and laugh at all of the funny things
that happen to us every day!"

Flora loved all of her family.
And she knew that they loved her, too.
"I may have dark hair, and yours is light,
but I'm still a big part of you.

"You look after me and protect me.
And you help me to learn and grow."
Flora smiled, then giggled, then
laughed loudly.

"I'm the happiest girl that I know!"

NOTES FOR PARENTS AND TEACHERS

- Look at the front cover of the book together. Talk about the picture. Can the children guess what the book is going to be about?

- Turn to pages 4–5. Bath time can be a fun, family time. Talk about how much fun Flora is having with her mom and dad. Invite the children to talk about their bath time fun.

- On page 7, Flora notices that her hair is long and dark, but that her mom's hair is short and light. Ask the children if they had noticed that, too.

- On pages 8–9, Flora's mom tells Flora that she has been adopted. Ask the children what they think it means to be adopted. Explain the meaning of adoption and answer any questions your children may have.

- Ask the children how they think Flora feels when she discovers she has been adopted. Do they know anyone who has been adopted?

- On page 10, Flora's mom and dad say how happy they are that Flora is part of their family. Ask the children how they think this makes Flora feel.

- On page 12, Flora asks if she is different from her brother and sister. Explain that adopted children are different in some ways (for example, they have different birth parents), but that they are the same in other ways (for example, they live in the same house, they have the same parents to take care of them, and they may like the same things).

- On page 14, Flora's dad says that babies need a lot of care. Invite the children to talk about the kind of care a baby needs. Explain that all children feel safest and happiest when they know that their parents can take care of all their needs. You could talk about this in terms of the parents being the "big ones," who do the looking after, and the children being the "little ones," who are looked after, so that they can grow and learn. Emphasize that all children, including adopted children, are the "little ones" in the family.

- On page 15, Flora's parents explain how hard it was for Flora's birth parents to decide to find an adoptive family for Flora. Discuss how this decision was made out of their love for her.

- On page 16, Flora worries that her birth parents did not keep her because she had done something wrong. This is a common concern for adopted children. Ask the children how they think Flora was feeling when she asked this question.

- On page 18, Flora's dad makes it clear that Flora's birth parents and her adoptive parents wanted to be sure that Flora felt loved and safe, and that she was taken care of. How do the children think Flora felt when she heard that?

- On page 20, Flora's mom says that it is good for Flora to ask a lot of questions. It is important for adopted children to know that they can ask as many questions as they want. Explain to the children that they can ask questions, and that, like Flora's mom and dad, you will always answer them so they can understand anything they need to know.

- On page 22, it is clear that Flora's family love each other very much. Ask the children what they think it is that makes Flora happy. Talk about what they have heard in the story that would cause Flora to be so happy.